BOUNDLESS HEART

Relationship advice for lasting love

LUNARISPEN

Title: BOUNDLESS HEART

Author: LUNARISPEN

Publication Year: 2024

For permission requests, contact the publisher at
ikhlafi1014@gmail.com

INTRODUCTION

"The history of humanity has been fashioned by the power of love. Numerous tales, from the grandiose tales of star-crossed lovers to the simple, enduring romances that take place in the cracks of ordinary life, are propelled by this force. Love is a journey full of unexpected turns, twists, and turns, full of infinite delight and significant problems. In order to understand the intricacies of the human heart, we set out on a trip to investigate the power of love and relationships in this book.

As this book's author, I offer you more than simply written words—I've taken you on a personal journey that has profoundly deepened my understanding of the infinite power of love. The stuff you are about to explore has been formed by my personal experiences and the lessons I have learned along the way. It is my goal that you will find meaning in my experiences and observations and that we may explore the realm of love and enduring happiness in relationships together.

Our journey begins right here, in the pages of this book, where we'll debunk the myths of ideal relationships and discover the power of authenticity, honesty, and open communication. We'll go into the depths of self-love and learn how it's the foundation of happiness in any relationship. We'll rekindle the spark of romance, dig into the beauty of sexual fulfillment, and investigate the function of emotional connection. We'll go through life's ups and downs and discover how to evolve as individuals within a committed partnership. The digital age brings with it its own set of issues and opportunities, and we'll look at how technology affects modern relationships, from online dating to social networking. We will welcome diversity and face any problems that may occur, such as cultural differences and motherhood trials. Finally, we will go on a trip into the golden years of love, sustaining the flame of desire and leaving a legacy of lasting love.

I cordially encourage you to accept my invitation to join me on this journey, opening your heart and mind to the infinite possibilities of love in all of its manifestations. Together, let's embark on this adventure, aiming to strengthen our bonds, draw lessons from our past, and commemorate the voyage of limitless hearts.

Chapter 1: Dissecting the Myth Around Relationships

Sub-chapter 1: Beyond Fairy Tales

In this sub-chapter, we will look at typical cultural fallacies about relationships, highlighting the need to accept the reality of ups and downs as well as the hazards of unreasonable expectations.

- **Challenging societal myths about perfect relationships**

Society frequently fosters the concept of "perfect" relationships, which is spread through many mediums such as fairy tales, movies, and social media. These stories frequently depict romantic relationships as perfect unions free of conflict or difficulty. However, such depictions fail to capture the complexities and hardships of real-world relationships.

- ## The Phenomenon of Variations in Actual Relationships

Contrary to popular belief, real relationships are not always easy to maintain. They include both pleasant and difficult situations, as well as highs and lows. Any partnership will inevitably include arguments, miscommunications, and confrontations. It is critical to recognize that these obstacles are not indicators of failure, but rather opportunities for growth and stronger relationships.

- ## The Dangers of Unrealistic Expectations

Unrealistic expectations based on social norms or media representations can be harmful to relationships. Believing in the idea of the perfect relationship can lead to discontent and disillusionment when reality fails to meet these unreasonable expectations. Couples may feel inadequate or uneasy if their relationship does not reflect the idealistic images they see. Thus, it is critical to debunk these beliefs and develop a more realistic view of what forms a healthy and fulfilling relationship.

Sub-chapter 2: The Power of Authenticity

This sub-chapter discusses the necessity of authenticity in relationships as well as the benefits of accepting yourself for who you truly are, creating trust through vulnerability, and finding beauty in defects.

• Consider relationships with your actual self

Genuine connections are based on authenticity. It requires remaining true to oneself and expressing honestly and openly about one's desires and emotions in a relationship. When people accept who they truly are, they inspire their connections to do the same, resulting in a welcoming and understanding environment. Conversely, stress and obedience can cause a relationship to become distant and resentful.

• Building trust through vulnerability

Vulnerability is frequently perceived as a weakness; however, it is an effective technique for developing trust and intimacy in relationships. Opening up about one's anxieties, insecurities, and vulnerabilities develops stronger bonds and enables partners to sympathize with and support one another. Trust grows when people feel comfortable enough to be vulnerable with one another, knowing that they will be met with empathy and acceptance.

- ## The beauty of imperfection

Perfection is an unrealistic goal that can stifle genuine connection and growth in relationships. Accepting defects, flaws, and blunders as part of the human experience promotes acceptance and compassion in the partnership. Couples can improve their bond by embracing imperfection, which fosters resilience, empathy, and understanding.

Sub-chapter 3: Open Communication and Honesty

In this sub-chapter, we look at the importance of honesty and open communication in developing strong and healthy relationships. We talk about overcoming communication hurdles and the value of attentive listening.

- ## Foundation of Strong Relationships

Honesty and open communication are essential for building effective partnerships. Being truthful and transparent in your relationship promotes trust, respect, and understanding. It fosters a climate in which both individuals feel comfortable expressing their views, feelings, and worries without fear of being judged or rejected.

• Overcoming Communication Barriers

Effective communication entails not only voicing your views but also actively listening to and empathizing with your partner's point of view. Common communication hurdles, such as defensiveness, criticism, and stonewalling, can inhibit understanding and exacerbate confrontations. Overcoming these obstacles necessitates empathy, tolerance, and a willingness to compromise.

• The Practice of Active Listening

Active listening is an essential ability for improving communication and strengthening relationships. It entails paying attention to what your partner is saying without interrupting or developing a response too soon. By paying close attention and empathizing with your partner's emotions, you display respect and validate their experiences, building a stronger connection and mutual understanding.

Sub-chapter 4: Handling Conflict with Grace

In this section, we'll look at how to handle arguments in a good way so that they become chances for growth and strengthen the bonds between the parties.

• Using Conflict as an Opportunity for Growth

Conflict is unavoidable in each relationship; nevertheless, how it is managed determines how long the partnership lasts and how well it functions. Couples can approach arguments with openness and curiosity when they regard them as opportunities for personal growth. Couples can increase their understanding of one another and build their relationship by addressing underlying issues and learning from disagreements.

• Successful Techniques for Conflict Resolution

To effectively resolve problems, you must be tolerant, compassionate, and willing to accept concessions. Use communication tactics such as "I" statements, active listening, and establishing common ground to have effective talks and prevent problems from worsening. Furthermore, giving people time to resolve disputes and grievances calmly and courteously helps to keep resentments at bay and trust intact.

● Reconciliation and healing injuries

Forgiveness is essential for both relationship maintenance and dispute resolution. Resentments and grudges can taint a relationship, preventing emotional intimacy. Couples can heal their relationship, regain trust, and move forward by practicing forgiveness and letting go of past hurts. Empathy, modesty, and a commitment to improving the relationship's foundation are required.

Sub-chapter 5: Establishing Intimacy and Trust

This subchapter discusses the importance of intimacy and trust in developing healthy, long-lasting partnerships.

● The Basis of Relationship Trust

Healthy relationships are founded on trust, which encompasses dependability, honesty, and integrity. When people trust their partner's reliability, they may be more open and sincere with them, resulting in a greater level of emotional closeness and connection. Establishing and maintaining open channels of communication requires consistency, honesty, and openness.

• Creating emotional and physical intimacy

Closeness and connection between partners are fostered by emotional and physical intimacy, which is why it's important in love partnerships. Physical intimacy includes proximity, love, and sexual expression; emotional intimacy is the candid sharing of ideas, emotions, and vulnerabilities. It takes priority to spend quality time together, have deep talks, and show affection regularly to cultivate closeness.

• Reestablishing contact with your spouse

Couples may drift apart during everyday life's chaos, which can cause feelings of alienation and loneliness. Prioritizing your partner's needs, interests, and wants while making time for shared experiences and activities is essential to reconnecting with them. Investing in the relationship improves the tie and rekindles the flame of intimacy, whether it is through

date nights, hobbies you both enjoy or meaningful
talks.

Chapter 2: Developing Love for Yourself to Create Healthier Connections

Sub-chapter 1: The Value of Self-Love

This subchapter investigates the critical role of self-love in promoting resilience, self-assurance, and overall well-being. We examine techniques for identifying and coping with self-doubt to foster self-compassion.

- **Self-love is the foundation of contentment**

Self-love is defined as constant acceptance and admiration for oneself. It is the cornerstone of contentment and fulfillment, allowing people to accept their defects, limitations, and abilities. Recognizing one's intrinsic value and prioritizing self-care practices that nourish the mind, body, and soul are critical steps toward building self-love.

- ## Recognizing and dealing with self-doubt

Self-doubt can destroy one's sense of self and limit one's ability to advance. This might manifest as imposter syndrome, negative self-talk, or fear of failure, and it prevents people from realizing their true potential. Self-awareness and rephrasing negative thought patterns through affirmations, mindfulness, and seeking assistance from trustworthy friends or professionals are required to overcome self-doubt.

- ## Accepting Your Compassion

Self-compassion means being compassionate, understanding, and forgiving toward oneself, particularly while confronting hardships or failing. It entails acknowledging our common humanity and the fact that everyone experiences problems and setbacks. People who practice self-compassion grow in resilience, reduce their tendency to criticize themselves and gain acceptance and inner tranquility.

Sub-chapter 2: Setting Boundaries

This section discusses the importance of defining and communicating sound individual limits within partnerships, as well as respecting your significant other's boundaries.

• Setting Mindful Personal Limits

Setting boundaries in a relationship is critical for identifying a person's distinct characteristics, needs, and limitations. They prevent feelings of resentment or stress and provide guidelines for proper behavior. To build healthy boundaries, a person must be able to voice their preferences, identify their distinct values, and, when necessary, stand up for themselves.

• Effective boundary communication

Setting and upholding limits in partnerships depends on effective communication. It is being firm and polite when communicating needs, wants, and boundaries. Partners can comprehend each other's boundaries and cooperate to make sure they are respected when there is clear and direct communication between them.

- **Respect your spouse's boundaries**

Establishing reciprocal respect, trust, and closeness in a relationship requires that you respect your partner's limits. It means not using force or manipulation and respecting their autonomy, preferences, and boundaries. Both partners can feel valued and appreciated in the relationship when limits are respected, which promotes a sense of safety and security.

Sub-chapter 3: Practices for Self-Care

This section discusses the necessity of self-care for emotional well-being, how to create a self-care regimen, and the link between self-care and stronger relationships.

Prioritizing self-care to improve emotional healthSelf-care encompasses activities and routines that promote and restore one's physical, mental, and emotional health. Making self-care a top priority is critical for maintaining balance, reducing stress, and preventing burnout. It comprises finding activities that make you happy, content, and calm, such as taking up a hobby, practicing mindfulness, or spending time outside.

- ## Creating a self-care schedule

Creating a consistent self-care routine makes it easier to incorporate self-nurturing habits into your daily life. This regimen can include exercise, meditation, journaling, and time spent with loved ones. Setting aside time for self-care helps people respect their health and develop the resilience required to face life's challenges.

- ## The Connection Between Improving Relationships and Self-Care

Self-care is important not only for one's health, but it also helps to strengthen interpersonal relationships. People who practice self-care have more energy, patience, and emotional stability, allowing them to be their best in relationships. People can approach relationships from a position of abundance rather than dependency by looking after themselves, which increases reciprocity and mutual respect.

Sub-chapter 4: Confidence and Self-Esteem

This section goes into ways to increase self-confidence in romantic relationships, overcome self-worth issues, and understand the impact of self-assurance on one's significant other.

• Enhancing Self-Belief in Partnerships

Being confident is both alluring and powerful; it encourages assertiveness, straightforward communication, and relational honesty. Developing confidence entails acknowledging one's talents, appreciating accomplishments, and overcoming self-limiting attitudes. People who are secure in themselves exude genuineness, which inspires appreciation and trust in their companions.

• Overcome self-esteem issues

Self-esteem difficulties can erode one's worth and impede interpersonal fulfillment. Overcoming low self-esteem needs self-awareness, self-compassion, and reframing negative self-perceptions. Engaging in self-affirming habits, seeking treatment, and surrounding oneself with supportive people can help one develop self-acceptance and confidence in relationships.

- ## Self-assurance and its Effect on Your Partner

Self-assurance has a great impact on the dynamics of a relationship, encouraging your spouse to feel secure, admire, and respect you. When people are secure in themselves, they exude charisma, genuineness, and emotional stability, which instills confidence and trust in their partners. Individuals who are confident in themselves are better able to negotiate problems, communicate their wants assertively, and contribute to a peaceful and rewarding relationship dynamic.

Sub-chapter 5: Letting Go of the Past

In this sub-chapter, we discuss the importance of moving on from former relationships, letting go of emotional baggage, and practicing forgiveness, especially forgiveness towards oneself.

- ## Giving Up Emotional Attachments to Past Relationships

If one carries emotional baggage from previous relationships, it may be difficult to grow individually and build meaningful friendships. To help let go of grudges, wrath, or grief, feelings must be acknowledged and processed, closure sought when appropriate, and the past reinterpreted as a teaching tool.

● Recovering and Proceeding

Nurturing self-compassion, forgiving others, and accepting personal growth are all necessary steps in recovering from previous hurts. Resilience can be developed and emotional healing facilitated by participating in therapeutic therapies like self-reflection, therapy, or creative expression. People make room for fresh starts and better relationships in the future by letting go of the past.

● The Practice of Self-Forgiveness in the Art of Forgiveness

Letting go of grudges and bitterness releases people from their burdens and is a transforming act. It entails putting aside resentment, accepting excuses, and letting go of the need for retribution. Furthermore, self-forgiveness is essential for developing self-compassion and personal development. People can develop inner peace and a positive self-image by admitting their mistakes, growing from them, and practicing self-forgiveness.

Chapter 3: Rediscovering Romance and Passion

Sub-chapter 1: The Evolution of Romance

This sub-chapter explores the evolution of romance in long-term partnerships, highlighting the significance of consistent romantic acts and maintaining the flame.

- ### Maintaining Romance in Long-Term Partnerships

In long-term partnerships, romance changes as a couple develops and strengthens their bond over time. A deeper, more profound kind of romance based on closeness, camaraderie, and shared experiences may replace the original spark, even though it may wane. Romance needs to be nourished by making time for each other, showing love and gratitude, and making consistent investments in the partnership.

• The Value of Consistently Romantic Motion

Frequent romantic gestures are vital for maintaining intimacy and connection in relationships. These actions could range from small acts of kindness and giving to big displays of affection and dedication. Whether it's planning a romantic dinner date, surprising your significant other with a beautiful note, or simply holding hands while strolling, these activities demonstrate love, gratitude, and effort, thereby strengthening the bond between couples.

• Maintaining the enthusiasm

In romantic relationships, passion is essential because it fosters connection, excitement, and desire. It takes work, imagination, and a willingness to explore new things to maintain the passion. By putting physical affection first, partaking in activities and hobbies together, and experimenting with new intimate connections, couples can rekindle their romance. Partners can maintain the fervor and continuously strengthen their relationship by accepting spontaneity and vulnerability.

Sub-chapter 2:Creative Date Ideas

This sub-chapter offers creative and unforgettable date-night suggestions to keep things fresh and exciting in your relationship.

• Creative and imaginative ideas for a date night

1- Cooking Class: Take a cooking class with a friend to learn how to make a new dish, which will inspire cooperation and creativity.

2- Outdoor Adventure: To experience nature and make enduring memories go hiking, camping, or kayaking.

3- Explore the arts by going to a museum, an art gallery, or a pottery class to see creation in action and gain fresh insights.

4- Stargazing Picnic: For a romantic evening among the stars, gather a blanket, and some refreshments, and head to a remote location.

5- Make Your Spa Night: Use candles, aromatherapy oils, and calming massages to create a tranquil spa atmosphere at home.

- ### Bringing the Flame Back with Unexpected Activities

1- Scavenger Hunt: To add excitement and adventure, organize a scavenger hunt with clues that lead to significant locations or shared experiences.

Surprise break: Rekindle the romance and discover new surroundings with your significant other by treating them to an impromptu weekend break at a nearby location.

2- Dance Class: Surprise your significant other by enrolling in a dance class together. This will help you get to know each other better and have fun while learning a new skill.

- ### Maintaining a sense of novelty in your relationship

1- Plan themed date nights, such as movie marathons, costume parties, or cultural adventures, to add excitement and diversity to your routine.

2- Bucket List Adventures: Make a list of activities you both want to do and commit to checking them off together, instilling a spirit of adventure and shared goals.

3- Volunteer Together: Set aside time to volunteer for a cause that you both care about, increasing your bond through shared beliefs and compassion.

Sub-chapter 3: The Role of Emotional Intimacy

This sub-chapter explores the importance of emotional intimacy in partnerships, emphasizing the importance of communicating dreams and worries, accepting vulnerability, and strengthening emotional bonds with your spouse.

- ## Building emotional bonds in partnerships

Emotional connectedness is the foundation for a strong and rewarding relationship. It requires forming a strong emotional bond with your spouse, knowing about their thoughts, feelings, and experiences, and offering empathy and support. Active listening, empathy, and the willingness to be open, honest, and vulnerable with your partner are all required to create a stronger emotional connection.

- ## The Intimacy of Vulnerability's Power

To promote emotional intimacy in partnerships, vulnerability is essential. It entails confiding in your spouse about your deepest worries, anxieties, and insecurities in the knowledge that they will be sympathetic and understanding. Accepting vulnerability makes it possible for couples to be more real and sincere while also fostering a deeper level of intimacy.

• Exchange of Fears and Dreams

A sense of mutual trust and support is fostered, and emotional intimacy is strengthened when a couple shares dreams and anxieties together. You can let your spouse into your inner world and communicate your hopes and worries by sharing your aims, goals, and fears with them. While discussing worries fosters dread, sharing dreams fosters a sense of shared purpose and excitement for the future.

Sub-chapter 4: Sexual Fulfillment

This section looks at how to cultivate a happy and healthy sexual connection with your significant other, including sharing your thoughts and wishes and resolving common sexual difficulties.

• Building a Positive Sexual Relationship with Your Partner

Sexual pleasure, an essential component of love relationships, promotes closeness, connection, and overall well-being. Respect for one another, open communication, and a willingness to explore and satisfy one another's goals and desires are all necessary for developing a strong sexual connection. During sexual interactions, it is critical to prioritize intimacy, pleasure, and emotional connection.

● Discussion of Fantasy and Desire

Sexual fulfillment and satisfaction necessitate efficient communication of dreams and wishes. Partners should be able to share their boundaries, fantasies, and sexual preferences in a friendly, nonjudgmental environment. Couples' intimacy and sexual connection can be increased by being open about their desires and attempting new things together.

● Overcoming typical sexual difficulties

Sexual problems are common in relationships and can be caused by a variety of factors, including interpersonal issues, stress, or weariness. Overcoming these challenges will require cooperation, tolerance, and understanding. Seeking expert help, engaging in mindfulness and relaxation techniques, and prioritizing emotional connection can all help with addressing sexual troubles and revitalizing intimacy in a relationship.

Sub-chapter 5: Keeping the Fun Alive

This section discusses the importance of incorporating humor and good humor in interpersonal relationships, cultivating mutual understanding and inside jokes, and maintaining a lighthearted mood even in the face of adversity.

• Bringing Humor and Playfulness into Your Relationship

Laughter and playfulness are essential components of a positive and healthy relationship. They make partnerships feel happier, carefree, and connected, which improves the ties and intimacy between partners. Playful activities that add excitement and novelty to the relationship, such as games, playful teasing, or spontaneous adventures, help to keep the spark alive.

• The Value of Inside Jokes and Personal Narratives

Partners feel more close and connected when they share jokes and experiences, which strengthens their bond and fosters a sense of community. They elicit affection and delight because they serve as reminders of special occasions and shared experiences. Establishing new shared experiences and inside jokes increases the emotional link and emphasizes the unique relationship between spouses.

● Being more positive in tough times

Stress and conflict in the relationship can be alleviated by maintaining a sense of humor and levity during difficult times. Humor provides perspective and relief from hardships and adversity, serving as a coping mechanism. Couples can overcome obstacles with fortitude and hope by embracing humor and lightheartedness, which will strengthen and deepen their relationship.

Chapter 4: Embracing Change and Growth Together

Sub-chapter 1: Embracing Life Transitions

In this section, we'll look at how to manage relationship changes, redefine connection amid change, and assist one another through difficult times.

• Handling Relationship Transitions

Transitions are common in life, from parenthood and marriage to retirement and empty nest syndrome. Effectively handling these adjustments in a partnership necessitates collaboration, communication, and mutual support. A couple must learn to recognize how changes affect their marital dynamics and work together to face these transformations with grace and perseverance.

• Reimagine Your Relationship with Changes

Couples can strengthen their devotion and rethink their relationship during transitions. Couples can try out new roles, behaviors, and experiences together by viewing change as a shared adventure. Accepting change fosters growth and strengthens resilience, allowing partners to shift and adapt to new situations while maintaining closeness and connection.

- ## **Providing Mutual Support During Tough Times**

A good and resilient relationship requires both sides to assist one another during difficult times. When dealing with health concerns, financial troubles, or personal crises, couples must rely on one another for understanding, encouragement, and emotional support. Partners can overcome difficulties and emerge stronger as a unit by providing understanding, affirmation, and constructive assistance.

Sub-chapter 2: Individual Growth in a Partnership

This section discusses the need to create a balance between individual development and dedicated collaboration, encourage one another's goals, and develop a shared future vision.

- ## Harmonizing Individual Development with a Dedicated Partnership

Mutual respect, communication, and compromise are required to establish a balance between a committed relationship and personal growth. While personal development and fulfillment are dependent on individual growth, the needs and goals of the relationship must also be given equal consideration. Couples must support each other's personal growth while maintaining a strong foundation of shared commitments, beliefs, and goals.

- ## Supporting one another's dreams and passions

Supporting one another's passions and aspirations strengthens the link and mutual support in a partnership. To help one another achieve their goals, partners should actively listen to each other's dreams, validate and encourage each other, and offer constructive suggestions. Partners promote an empowerment and growth culture by praising and celebrating one another's efforts.

- ## Creating a common future vision

Developing a shared future vision is the first step toward a fruitful and fulfilling collaboration. To connect their future thoughts, couples should have open discussions about their beliefs, long-term goals, and objectives. Couples can attain mutual goals, make plans together, and support one another's ambitions.

Sub-chapter 3: Resilience in Relationships

This sub-chapter discusses the importance of building resilience in relationships, as well as how to overcome barriers and, if necessary, reinvent the partnership.

• Increasing your partnership's resilience in the face of adversity

Resilience is defined as the ability to persevere through adversity and emerge stronger on the other side. Relationship resilience is fostered by effective communication, mutual trust, and support. Couples can boost their resilience by working together to overcome hurdles, devising creative solutions, and recovering from setbacks.

- ## Adapting to the Unpredictability of Life and External Stressors

Even the strongest relationships can experience strain from external stressors since life is unpredictable. It takes perseverance, adaptability, and a willingness to lower expectations to react to these pressures. To handle life's ups and downs with resilience and grace, couples must work together, be open and honest with one another about their needs and feelings, and support and understand one another.

- ## Reimagining the Bond When Required

Relationships may need to alter and adjust to new dynamics as people and situations do. To reinvent the connection, one must consider their common beliefs, objectives, and aspirations, as well as possible strategies for realigning and reviving the alliance. Couples can reinvent their relationship to guarantee its continuous growth and development by accepting change, being open with one another, and being willing to consider new options.

Sub-chapter 4: Rekindling Friendship

This sub-chapter emphasizes the importance of keeping friendships outside of romantic relationships, rekindling the companionship that first brought people together, and spending quality time with friends.

• Restoring the Value of Friendship in Your Partnership

Friendship serves as the foundation for a strong and lasting love connection. Rekindling a friendship includes developing camaraderie, mutual respect, and trust while also enjoying each other's company. Couples should prioritize meaningful interactions, laughter, and shared interests to improve their relationship and make it more meaningful.

• Regaining the Friendship That First Brought You Both Together

It's important to review past encounters, inside jokes, and moments that encouraged intimacy and connection to rekindle the companionship that first drew couples together. To rekindle their friendship and companionship, couples should remember their early days of dating, partake in activities they both enjoy and make new memories together.

- **Being friends and spending quality time together**

Friendships require closeness and connection, which can only be sustained by spending meaningful time together. Activities that foster bonding, including going on walks, cooking together, or playing games, should be given priority by couples. Couples can rekindle their sense of humor and enjoyment in their relationship and fortify their emotional bond by setting aside time specifically for friendship and companionship.

Sub-chapter 5: Celebrating Milestones and Memories

In this sub-chapter, we talk about the importance of commemorating events and memories in a relationship, creating customs and rituals, and reflecting on prior experiences to commemorate the journey that partners have traveled together.

- ## Keeping a record of specific times throughout your joint journey

Recognizing and valuing the journey that partners have taken necessitates commemorating life milestones such as birthdays, anniversaries, and achievements. Couples can remember these special milestones with emotional gestures, thoughtful presents, or amazing experiences to demonstrate how much they respect and appreciate each other's presence in their lives.

- ## Forming customs and rituals

Rituals and customs help to create a sense of continuity and connection in a partnership. Couples can establish routines such as weekly check-ins, date nights, and holiday traditions to strengthen their relationship and build togetherness. These practices deepen the link between the two people by providing opportunities for interaction, reflection, and celebration.

- ## Reflecting on Your Common Past to Appreciate the Adventure You've Had

When a couple reflects on their shared history, they may see the growth, resilience, and love that have sustained their relationship over time. Partners must take time to reflect on significant experiences, challenges overcome, and mutual achievements. Couples build their emotional link by reaffirming their commitment to each other's enjoyment and well-being.

Chapter 5: Nurturing Love in the Digital Age

Sub-chapter 1: Modern Challenges and Opportunities

In this sub-chapter, we look at how technology affects modern relationships, the potential benefits and cons of digital technologies, and the frequent mistakes to avoid in the digital age.

- ### How Technology Affects Modern Relationships

Technology has transformed how we communicate, connect, and engage with people, including love partners. While it provides unprecedented convenience and accessibility, it also presents new problems and complications in relationships. From continual connectivity to social media influence, technology has a tremendous impact on the dynamics of modern relationships.

Digital Instruments to Boost Interaction and Conversation

Technology offers chances to improve connection and communication in relationships, even despite its drawbacks. Whatever their physical distance, couples may communicate, coordinate, and work together in real-time thanks to digital tools like shared calendars, video calls, and messaging applications. Online forums and social media platforms also offer ways to communicate with loved ones, express affection, and share experiences.

• Typical Errors in the Digital Era to Sidestep

Though ubiquitous in our lives, technology can also result in common mistakes that compromise the closeness and quality of our relationships. Digital distractions during quality time spent together, excessive screen time, and misunderstandings or miscommunications brought on by dependence on digital communication are a few examples. To successfully navigate the digital world, one must be aware of these hazards.

Sub-chapter 2: Healthy Digital Boundaries

This section of the book discusses ways to set realistic limitations on technology use in relationships, striking a balance between social and screen time, and unplugging to reconnect with your spouse.

- ## Setting limits on the use of technology in relationships

Setting boundaries for technology use is critical for maintaining a harmonious and balanced relationship. Couples should openly discuss their preferences, concerns, and expectations regarding technology use and work together to establish boundaries that respect each other's needs and interests. This could include mutual respect for one another's privacy and personal space, established screen usage limits, and designated tech-free zones or periods.

- ## Techniques for Balancing Social and Screen Time

To foster intimacy and connection in a relationship, screen time and social time should be balanced. Prioritizing meaningful conversations, sharing activities, or simply enjoying meals together should all occur during quality time spent away from digital distractions. Partners can strengthen their relationship by being more aware of one another's needs and giving each other greater attention.

- ## Disconnecting to reconnect with your partner.

Disconnecting from technology regularly allows couples to reconnect on a deeper level and strengthen their emotional bond. Disconnecting from digital devices, whether on date nights, weekends away, or vacations, allows for actual connection, intimacy, and presence. Partners may foster a relationship that lasts beyond the digital realm by prioritizing face-to-face interaction and meaningful experiences.

Sub-chapter 3: Online Dating and Long-Distance Love

In this sub-chapter, we look at the complexities of online dating, how to maintain long-distance relationships in the digital era, and how to create trust and communicate effectively online.

• Navigating the World of Online Dating

Online dating has grown in popularity in modern culture, allowing people to communicate with potential companions regardless of geography. To navigate the world of online dating, you must first create an authentic profile, then engage in meaningful chats, and finally exercise care while examining prospective matches. It's critical to go into online dating with realistic expectations and prioritize safety and consent throughout the process.

• Maintaining Long-Distance Relationships in the Digital Era

Long-distance relationships require deliberate effort and efficient communication to succeed in the digital age. Couples can stay connected and intimate despite physical distance by using technology such as video calls, messaging applications, and virtual dates. Maintaining a long-distance relationship requires emphasizing frequent communication, cultivating trust and emotional connection, and devising inventive ways to bridge the gap between visits.

- ### **Successful Online Communication and trust-building**

Effective online communication is critical for establishing trust and connection in both online dating and long-distance relationships. Couples should value open and honest communication, active listening, and vulnerability in their interactions. Partners can build trust, develop emotional connections, and lay a solid foundation for their relationship by discussing their thoughts, feelings, and experiences truthfully.

Sub-chapter 4: Dealing with Social Media and Jealousy

This section discusses strategies for dealing with envy and insecurity in the age of social media, fostering transparency and confidence in social media conversations, and engaging in digital detoxing to keep a positive dynamic in a relationship.

- ### **Managing Insecurity and Jealousy in the Social Media Era**

Comparisons, perceived threats, and imprecise connections on social media can exacerbate emotions of insecurity and jealousy inside partnerships. Managing envy requires growing self-awareness, and trust, and resolving underlying problems through honest discussion and empathy. Setting limitations on social media use, valuing in-person contacts, and focusing on maintaining stability and trust in their relationship are all sound suggestions for couples.

• Trust and Transparency in Social Media Exchanges

In social media conversations, fostering trust and security requires openness and honesty. Couples need to stay in constant contact regarding their social media usage, including messaging, friend connections, and online interactions. In addition to reducing envy, partners can foster mutual trust and understanding by being open and honest about their online presence and honoring each other's boundaries.

• Digital Reduction Techniques to Preserve a Positive Relationship

Couples can prioritize spending time together and strengthen their bond away from screens and other distractions by engaging in a digital detox. Couples may concentrate on one another, have deep talks, and make enduring memories by scheduling specific tech-free hours or weekends. Couples can improve their relationship, lower stress levels, and foster a healthier lifestyle by occasionally unplugging electronics.

Sub-chapter 5: Using Technology for Connection

This section digs into creative ways to use technology to strengthen marital relationships, transmit affection through digital channels, and maintain closeness even when physically apart.

• Using Technology to Improve Your Relationships

Technology provides numerous opportunities for couples to strengthen and grow their relationship. Despite being physically separated or having hectic schedules, couples can use technology to stay in touch and be involved in each other's lives by exchanging loving messages, sharing photographs, planning virtual dates, and playing online games. Partners can use technology to create an intimate and cohesive virtual community by prioritizing meaningful connections and high-quality interactions.

- ## Innovative Ways to Use Digital to Express Love

Couples can stay intimate and connected even when they are physically apart by expressing their love and affection digitally. Digital love may be conveyed in a variety of creative ways, like sending virtual love notes, creating shared playlists, and sending video messages. Partners can strengthen their connections and rekindle their commitment by utilizing technology to create unique and intimate ways to interact.

- ## Technology's Function in Maintaining Closeness Even When Physically Distant

Technology is vital for keeping partners connected and close, especially when they are geographically apart. Couples can share their experiences, sentiments, and everyday life events in real-time via video chats, voice messages, and social media platforms, fostering a sense of presence and unity.

Chapter 6: Embracing Diversity and Overcoming Challenges

Sub-chapter 1: Cultural Differences and Relationships

In this sub-chapter, we look at how couples can negotiate relationships with partners from various cultural origins, celebrate cultural variety, and promote communication and understanding in intercultural partnerships.

• Managing Relationships with Partners from Different Backgrounds

Managing relationships with partners from various cultural origins necessitates sensitivity, open-mindedness, and respect for differences. Couples should actively discuss their cultural backgrounds, traditions, and values, attempting to understand and accept each other's perspectives. Partners can improve and strengthen their relationship by acknowledging and accepting cultural differences.

- ## Celebrate the Richness of Cultural Diversity in Your Relationship

Cultural diversity improves relationships by bringing different ideas, traditions, and experiences to the table. Couples should celebrate ethnic variety by learning about each other's customs, cuisines, and festivities. Accepting variety develops reciprocal respect, appreciation, and curiosity, resulting in a vibrant and dynamic partnership that recognizes and values each partner's cultural history.

- ## Communication and understanding in multicultural relationships

Effective communication is essential for managing cultural differences and cultivating understanding in intercultural interactions. Couples should prioritize clear and empathic communication, actively listening to and validating each other's perspectives. Partners can overcome cultural barriers and develop relationships based on empathy and mutual understanding by cultivating an open and respectful atmosphere.

Sub-chapter 2: Overcoming Relationship Challenges

This sub-chapter discusses ways for detecting and addressing typical relationship obstacles, dealing with concerns such as infidelity and trust, and obtaining professional treatment when necessary.

• Identifying and Addressing Common Relationship Challenges

Relationships will inevitably face difficulties, ranging from communication issues and conflict to external stressors and life upheavals. Identifying and addressing these difficulties necessitates self-awareness, open reflection, and proactive communication. Couples should work together to discover underlying difficulties, freely address their concerns, and collaborate to develop solutions that will strengthen their relationship.

• Strategies for Managing Infidelity, Trust Issues, and Other Difficulties

Infidelity, trust issues, and other serious problems can have a significant impact on a relationship's health and stability. Taking on these issues demands courage, patience, and a dedication to healing and reconciliation. Couples should prioritize transparency, accountability, and forgiveness when dealing with infidelity and regaining trust. Seeking couples therapy or expert advice can help you navigate these complicated issues and restore the foundation of your relationship.

- ## Seeking professional help when needed

Relationship problems can feel overwhelming or beyond the reach of self-help solutions. In such instances, obtaining professional assistance can help resolve disagreements, and restore relationships. Couples therapy provides a secure and supportive environment in which couples can discuss their concerns, gain effective communication skills, and devise solutions for overcoming barriers. Couples can endure adversities and emerge stronger together by prioritizing their relationship's well-being and getting support as needed.

Sub-chapter 3: Nurturing a Relationship After Children

In this sub-chapter, we look at ways to balance parenthood while maintaining a loving relationship, build co-parenting unity, and keep the romance alive as parents.

• Balancing Parenting and Maintaining a Loving Relationship

Balancing the obligations of children and building a healthy relationship necessitates deliberate effort and focus. Couples should make time for each other amidst the demands of parenting, whether by setting regular date nights, engaging in meaningful talks, or just expressing gratitude for each other's efforts. Prioritizing quality time together allows spouses to develop their bond and maintain their connection despite the pleasures and hardships of parenting children.

• Co-parenting and Maintaining a Unified Front

Effective co-parenting entails maintaining a united front and working as a team to support one another and satisfy the needs of the children. Couples should talk openly about parenting tactics, duties, and obligations and collaborate to address issues and make decisions that benefit the entire family. Partners can deepen their connection by encouraging mutual respect, cooperation, and consistency in co-parenting.

- ### **Keeping Romance Alive as Parents**

Maintaining romance amidst the pressures of parenthood necessitates creativity, spontaneity, and a desire to value intimacy and connection. Couples should find methods to incorporate romance into their daily lives, such as surprising each other with little gestures of affection, organizing romantic getaways, or trying new activities together. By cultivating passion and intimacy, spouses can reignite the flame of romance and expand their bond as they navigate the joys and challenges of parenthood together.

Sub-chapter 4: Supporting Each Other's Goals

This sub-chapter discusses the significance of encouraging mutual support for each other's goals, balancing career goals and personal progress with the partnership, and celebrating individual accomplishments together.

- ### **Promoting Mutual Support for Each Other's Aspirations**

Supporting each other's aims and aspirations is critical to developing a strong and fulfilling relationship. Couples should actively listen to each other's goals and desires, offer encouragement and support, and celebrate each other's accomplishments. Partners who are one another's biggest supporters can establish a supportive environment that promotes personal growth and improves their bond.

- **Managing professional goals and personal development in a relationship**

Effective communication, willingness to compromise, and mutual respect are necessary while juggling professional goals and personal development in a partnership. Open communication about objectives, aspirations, and career goals is essential for couples. They should also work together to discover ways to support one another's professional endeavors without sacrificing their relationship. Partners can pursue their respective ambitions while putting the health of their partnership first by striking a healthy balance between work and personal life.

- ## Together, we celebrate each other's successes

Celebrating individual accomplishments together deepens the relationship between couples and reaffirms their dedication to one another's prosperity and happiness. Couples should be proud of and enthusiastic about each other's successes, whether they are following a passion project, getting a new job, or hitting personal milestones.

Sub-chapter 5: Staying Resilient During Life's Storms

In this sub-chapter, we will look at ways of dealing with illness, sorrow, and other life issues as a partnership, as well as how to develop a support network for both partners and maintain love and connection during difficult times.

- ## Coping with Illness, Grief, and Other Life Challenges for Couples

Coping with illness, sorrow, and other life obstacles can put a strain on a relationship and test its strength. Couples should talk frankly about their emotions, anxieties, and wants, as well as provide unconditional support and comfort to one another.

By addressing obstacles as a team, couples can manage difficult times with fortitude and unity, deepening their bond in the process.

• Creating a Support Network for Both Partners

Creating a support network of friends, family, and trusted experts is essential for offering emotional and practical help to both spouses during difficult times. Couples should seek counsel, encouragement, and assistance from their support network, as well as provide unshakable support and empathy to one another. Partners can weather life's storms together by forming a solid support system.

• Strengthening Your Love and Connection Throughout Adversity

To strengthen love and connection during difficult times, patience, understanding, and dedication to each other's well-being are required. Couples should prioritize spending quality time together, doing things that make them happy and comfortable, and freely and frequently expressing their love and gratitude for one another. Partners who face hardships together and rely on each other for support can emerge from adversity with a deeper appreciation for their partnership as well as a revitalized sense of strength and resilience.

Chapter 7: Thriving in the Golden Years of Love

Sub-chapter 1: Nurturing Love After Decades Together

In this sub-chapter, we will look at ways of sustaining love and passion in long-term partnerships, appreciating the wisdom and shared history of enduring love, and rediscovering one another in our golden years.

- **Maintaining love and passion in long-term relationships**

Maintaining love and passion in long-term partnerships needs intentionality, work, and a willingness to change together over time. Couples should stress intimacy, communication, and mutual respect while actively cultivating their emotional bond and physical affection. Partners may keep the spark of passion alive over time by accepting change, sharing new experiences, and prioritizing each other's wants and desires.

- ## **Celebrate the wisdom and shared history of enduring love**

Celebrating the wisdom and shared history of long-lasting love allows couples to reflect on their journey together and appreciate the depth and richness of their relationship. Partners should treasure the memories, achievements, and problems they've faced, acknowledging their relationship's strength and tenacity. Couples strengthen their bond and renew their dedication to each other's happiness and well-being by paying tribute to their shared history with gratitude and reverence.

- ## **Rediscovering each other in our golden years**

The golden years provide an opportunity for couples to rediscover each other and reconnect in fresh and meaningful ways. Partners should embrace the freedom and flexibility that come with older age, discovering new interests and hobbies, and traveling together. By remaining curious, open-minded, and adventurous, couples can rediscover the excitement and joy of falling in love all over again, resulting in a partnership that evolves and flourishes throughout time.

Sub-chapter 2: Maintaining a Sense of Independence

In this sub-chapter, we look at ways to balance togetherness with personal independence in later life, following separate interests and hobbies, and reigniting the spark in adult partnerships.

• Balancing Togetherness and Personal Freedom in Later Life

Balancing togetherness with personal freedom in older life necessitates open communication, mutual respect, and a fair amount of independence. Couples should recognize and respect each other's needs for space, autonomy, and self-expression, while also strengthening their link and connection. Partners can develop a relationship that combines closeness and personal fulfillment by setting boundaries, maintaining separate interests, and supporting each other's progress.

• Pursuing individual interests and hobbies

Pursuing individual interests and hobbies enriches both spouses' lives while also encouraging personal development and contentment. Couples should encourage each other to pursue their passions and discover new interests, whether it's starting a new activity, pursuing lifelong goals, or embarking on solo travel. By encouraging each other's hobbies, partners foster independence, self-discovery, and a greater appreciation for each other's uniqueness.

- ## Reviving the Spark in Your Mature Relationship

Rekindling the spark in a mature relationship needs creativity, spontaneity, and a willingness to accept change. Couples should prioritize romance, intimacy, and playfulness and try to surprise and excite each other frequently. Whether it's planning romantic holidays, experiencing new experiences together, or simply enjoying each other's company in quiet moments, couples may reignite the spark of passion and keep their love alive into their golden years.

Sub-chapter 3: Legacy and Creating Family Traditions

In this sub-chapter, we look at the necessity of passing down wisdom and values to future generations, family rituals, and sustaining the love narrative.

- ## Passing down wisdom and values to the next generation

Passing on wisdom and beliefs to the next generation is an important way to leave a lasting legacy and contribute to the future. Couples should reflect on their life experiences, lessons acquired, and personal values and actively share this knowledge with their children and grandchildren. By sharing stories, thoughts, and guidance, partners may establish a sense of identity, resilience, and purpose in future generations, ensuring that their legacy lasts for years.

- ## The importance of family rituals and making lasting memories

Family rituals and traditions serve an important role in instilling a sense of belonging, identity, and connection among generations. Couples should create significant rituals and traditions that honor their love, values, and milestones, such as annual family trips, Christmas traditions, and weekly family dinners. These rituals allow for bonding, laughter, and shared experiences, building a long-lasting sense of family unity and cohesion.

- ## Preserving Your Love Story for the Future

By preserving your love story for future generations, couples can share their journey and legacy with their descendants. Couples should chronicle their love story in journals, photos, or recorded conversations, recording the milestones, hardships, and successes that have changed their relationship throughout time. Partners who preserve their love story in physical ways leave a meaningful legacy that inspires and uplifts future generations, reminding them of the enduring power of love and dedication.

Sub-chapter 4: Supporting Each Other's Well-Being

In this sub-chapter, we look at ways to promote physical and emotional health in later life, cope with aging, and embrace reciprocal care and affection.

- ## Encourage physical and emotional health in your later years

Promoting physical and emotional health is critical for preserving well-being in the later years of life. To improve physical health and vitality, couples should prioritize frequent exercise, a healthy diet, and stress-management skills. Furthermore, encouraging open communication, active listening, and emotional support improves mental and emotional health, creating a supportive environment in which both partners can thrive.

• Coping with Aging and Accepting the Changes Together

Coping with aging entails accepting change with grace and fortitude and addressing obstacles as a group. Couples should accept the natural changes that come with aging, whether they be physical restrictions, health difficulties, or lifestyle changes, and support one another with compassion and understanding. Partners can handle the later years with resilience and strength if they face aging together and adjust to new situations.

• Mutual Care and Companionship during the Golden Years

Mutual care and companionship are critical for prospering in the senior years of life. Couples should emphasize quality time together, participate in shared activities that offer them joy and contentment, and foster a sense of intimacy and connection.

Sub-chapter 5: Preparing for the Future

In this sub-chapter, we look at legal and financial planning, retirement, and maintaining peace of mind and contentment in your golden years.

• Legal and Financial Issues for Later Life

Preparing for the future means taking legal and financial precautions to assure security and peace of mind in later years. Couples should work with legal and financial specialists to draft or update crucial documents like wills, trusts, and advance directives, as well as develop a complete retirement plan that reflects their goals and beliefs. By taking proactive actions to protect their financial future, spouses can enjoy peace of mind and security as they enter their golden years together.

• Plan for Retirement and Long-Term Care

Planning for retirement and long-term care is critical for preserving freedom and quality of life in later life. Couples should assess their retirement assets, investments, and insurance coverage and devise a strategy for paying for their lifestyle and future healthcare needs in retirement. Furthermore, addressing long-term care preferences and options, such as aging in place or assisted living, ensures that partners are prepared for any future unforeseen circumstances and can make informed decisions together.

- ## **Promoting Peace of Mind and Contentment in the Golden Years**

Cultivating thankfulness, acceptance, and a sense of purpose in one's golden years is essential for promoting peace of mind and contentment. Couples should live in the present moment, relishing the little pleasures and experiences that provide fulfillment and happiness. By cultivating meaningful relationships, pursuing passions and interests, and embracing age-related insights, spouses can build a sense of calm, satisfaction, and fulfillment that will enrich their golden years together.

Chapter 8: A Lifelong Journey of Boundless Hearts

Sub-chapter 1: Reflecting on Your Relationship's Evolution

In this sub-chapter, we discuss the necessity of reflecting on your relationship's growth and transformation, appreciating the problems you've overcome together, and expressing thanks and love for your shared journey.

- **Looking back at the growth and transformation of your relationship**

Reflecting on the development and evolution of your relationship allows you to recognize how far you've come as a pair. Take time to reflect on the milestones, challenges, and unforgettable experiences that have formed your journey together. Celebrate your progress and the lessons you've learned along the way, and recognize the tenacity and strength that have propelled your partnership forward.

- ## Recognize the challenges you've conquered together

Recognize the problems you've overcome together as proof of your resilience and dedication. Recognize how you've supported each other and become stronger as a result of navigating conflicts and overcoming hurdles, as well as weathering life's storms. By admitting and honoring the difficulties you've encountered, you reaffirm the strength of your bond and your partnership's ability to overcome hardship.

- ## Expressing gratitude and love for your shared journey

Express your thanks and love for the wonderful adventure you've taken together. Take the time to recognize and appreciate the love, support, and companionship that your partner has contributed over the years. Whether via genuine talks, loving letters, or significant gestures, express your gratitude for the blessings and joys that your relationship has offered you.

Sub-chapter 2: Renewing Commitment and Vows

In this sub-chapter, we look at the importance of renewing your commitment to each other, confirming your love and future pledges, and using rituals and ceremonies to strengthen your bond.

• Celebrating your commitment to each other in a new way.

Celebrate your devotion to each other in a new way by renewing your vows or recommitting to your relationship. Plan a unique ceremony or intimate gathering to commemorate this significant milestone in your partnership. Whether you're exchanging new vows, confirming your love in front of loved ones, or sharing significant vows in private, use this occasion to celebrate the depth and strength of your relationship.

• Reaffirming Your Love and Promise for the Future

As you renew your commitment to one another, reaffirm your love and make future pledges. Take time to reflect on your shared path and the goals you hope to achieve together. Share your future goals, plans, and intentions, confirming your commitment to supporting and growing together as a pair.

- ## Rituals and Ceremonies for Renewing Your Bond

Consider integrating rituals and ceremonies to strengthen your tie and connection. Rituals, such as exchanging rings, lighting candles, or speaking significant vows, can represent the renewal of your commitment and the strength of your relationship. Choose rituals that are meaningful to both of you and represent your values and objectives.

Sub-chapter 3: Passing Down Wisdom

In this sub-chapter, we look at the value of sharing your relationship lessons with others, becoming relationship mentors for the next generation, and leaving a lasting legacy of love and understanding.

- ## Sharing Your Relationship Perspectives With Others

Sharing your relationship insights with others is a valuable way to provide advice, support, and encouragement to those embarking on their romantic adventures. Sharing your experiences, whether through storytelling, mentorship, or advice, can bring useful perspectives and life lessons. By sharing your experiences and expertise, you inspire others to create healthy, satisfying relationships of their own.

• Become Relationship Mentors for the Next Generation

Becoming a relationship mentor for the next generation allows you to pass on your expertise, values, and talents to younger couples looking for guidance and support. Offer your time, expertise, and support to couples in your neighborhood or family circle, giving them the tools and insights they need to negotiate the intricacies of love and partnership. By serving as role models and mentors, you encourage others to develop strong, resilient relationships based on trust, communication, and mutual respect.

• Leaving a Legacy of Love and Understanding

Leaving a lasting legacy of love and understanding is a powerful method to improve the well-being and happiness of future generations. By embodying and modeling good relationship dynamics, you generate a ripple effect of love and understanding that lasts well beyond your lifetime. Your loving legacy acts as a beacon of hope and inspiration for future generations, encouraging more empathy, compassion, and connectedness around the world.

Sub-chapter 4: Your Ongoing Love Story

In this sub-chapter, we will look at the importance of enjoying the ongoing adventure of love and connection, continuing to explore, learn, and develop together, and your responsibility to preserve the infinite heart of your partnership.

- ## Embracing the ongoing adventure of love and connection

Accept the continual journey of love and connection by entering each day with curiosity, openness, and joy. Consider your partnership a voyage of discovery and exploration, with limitless chances for growth, connection, and shared experiences. By accepting the unknown and remaining open to new possibilities, you maintain the spark of excitement and wonder in your relationship.

- ### Continue to explore, learn, and grow together

Continuing to explore, learn, and grow together is critical to keeping your relationship alive and blooming. Commit to lifelong study and personal development, both individually and as a pair. Seek out new experiences, challenges, and adventures that will push you beyond your comfort zone and enhance your connection. By remaining curious, adaptable, and committed to mutual improvement, you can foster a connection that evolves and thrives over time.

- ### Your role in maintaining the boundless heart of your relationship

Recognize your responsibility in keeping your relationship's infinite heart alive by cultivating love, compassion, and understanding in all of your encounters. Actively build a culture of love, admiration, and respect in your relationship, focusing on empathy, communication, and forgiveness. By cultivating a sense of safety, acceptance, and belonging, you create an environment in which love can develop and flourish, enhancing both your own and others' lives.

Conclusion

This book has taken us on a trip to examine the complexities of relationships, from dispelling misconceptions to cultivating love in the digital era and surviving in the golden years. As we come to the end of our journey, let us consider the important takeaways and how they can have a significant impact on our lives and relationships.

For starters, we've learned to confront conventional clichés and accept the realities of partnerships, acknowledging that flaws and struggles are natural and can improve our commitment. We've looked at how authenticity, honesty, and open communication may create trust and intimacy, as well as how to handle disagreements gracefully while establishing closeness and trust.

We've discussed the importance of self-love, setting boundaries, and practicing self-care for emotional well-being, realizing that loving oneself is the foundation of happiness and good relationships. We've also looked at the evolution of romance, the function of emotional connection, and the value of having fun while realizing that love takes constant effort and maintenance.

As we move forward, let us be encouraged to apply the ideas and insights obtained from this book to our relationships. Let us remember that true happiness in partnerships necessitates continual work, communication, and dedication. By putting love, understanding, and mutual respect first, we may build relationships that bring us joy, fulfillment, and significance.

Dear reader, I want to express my heartfelt gratitude for your joining me on this journey. I hope that the information imparted on these pages inspires your unlimited heart and your connections to bloom. May you find strength, courage, and joy in your quest for love and happiness, and may your path be filled with numerous moments of love, laughter, and connection.

Finally, remember that love is a lifelong adventure full of twists and turns and highs and lows. But, through it all, may we take comfort in knowing that love can transform, heal, and provide limitless joy. May we accept each moment gratefully and take every opportunity to love sincerely and live fully.

Best wishes for a lifetime of love and happiness.
LUNARISPEN